The Story of Edward Howard *and* the First American Watch

British Library Cataloguing-in-Publication Data
A catalogue record for this book is available from the British Library

A History of Clocks and Watches

Horology (from the Latin, Horologium) is the science of measuring time. Clocks, watches, clockwork, sundials, clepsydras, timers, time recorders, marine chronometers and atomic clocks are all examples of instruments used to measure time. In current usage, horology refers mainly to the study of mechanical time-keeping devices, whilst chronometry more broadly included electronic devices that have largely supplanted mechanical clocks for accuracy and precision in time-keeping. Horology itself has an incredibly long history and there are many museums and several specialised libraries devoted to the subject. Perhaps the most famous is the *Royal Greenwich Observatory,* also the source of the Prime Meridian (longitude 0° 0' 0"), and the home of the first marine timekeepers accurate enough to determine longitude.

The word 'clock' is derived from the Celtic words *clagan* and *clocca* meaning 'bell'. A silent instrument missing such a mechanism has traditionally been known as a timepiece, although today the words have become interchangeable. The clock is one of the oldest human interventions, meeting the need to consistently measure intervals of time shorter than the natural units: the day, the lunar month and the year. The current sexagesimal system of time measurement dates to approximately 2000 BC in Sumer. The Ancient Egyptians divided the day into two twelve-hour periods and used large obelisks to track the movement of the sun. They also developed water clocks, which had also been employed frequently by the Ancient Greeks, who called them 'clepsydrae'. The Shang Dynasty is also believed to have used the outflow water clock around the same time.

The first mechanical clocks, employing the verge escapement mechanism (the mechanism that controls the rate of a clock by advancing the gear train at regular intervals or 'ticks') with a foliot or balance wheel timekeeper (a weighted wheel that rotates back and forth, being returned toward its centre position by a spiral), were invented in Europe at around the start of the fourteenth century. They became the standard timekeeping device until the pendulum clock was invented in 1656. This remained the most accurate timekeeper until the 1930s, when quartz oscillators (where the mechanical resonance of a vibrating crystal is used to create an electrical signal with a very precise frequency) were invented, followed by atomic clocks after World War Two. Although initially limited to laboratories, the development of microelectronics in the 1960s made quartz clocks both compact and cheap to produce, and by the 1980s they became the world's dominant timekeeping technology in both clocks and wristwatches.

The concept of the wristwatch goes back to the production of the very earliest watches in the sixteenth century. Elizabeth I of England received a wristwatch from Robert Dudley in 1571, described as an arm watch. From the beginning, they were almost exclusively worn by women, while men used pocket-watches up until the early twentieth century. This was not just a matter of fashion or prejudice; watches of the time were notoriously prone to fouling from exposure to the elements, and could only reliably be kept safe from harm if carried securely in the pocket. Wristwatches were first worn by military men towards the end of the nineteenth century, when the importance of synchronizing manoeuvres during war without potentially revealing the plan to the enemy through signalling was increasingly recognized. It was clear that using pocket watches while in the heat of battle or while mounted on a horse was impractical, so officers began to strap the watches to their wrist.

The company H. Williamson Ltd., based in Coventry, England, was one of the first to capitalize on this opportunity. During the company's 1916 AGM it was noted that '...the public is buying the practical things of life. Nobody can truthfully contend that the watch is a luxury. It is said that one soldier in every four wears a wristlet watch, and the other three mean to get one as soon as they can.' By the end of the War, almost all enlisted men wore a wristwatch, and after they were demobilized, the fashion soon caught on - the British *Horological Journal* wrote in 1917 that '...the wristlet watch was little used by the sterner sex before the war, but now is seen on the wrist of nearly every man in uniform and of many men in civilian attire.' Within a decade, sales of wristwatches had outstripped those of pocket watches.

Now that clocks and watches had become 'common objects' there was a massively increased demand on clockmakers for maintenance and repair. Julien Le Roy, a clockmaker of Versailles, invented a face that could be opened to view the inside clockwork – a development which many subsequent artisans copied. He also invented special repeating mechanisms to improve the precision of clocks and supervised over 3,500 watches. The more complicated the device however, the more often it needed repairing. Today, since almost all clocks are now factory-made, most modern clockmakers *only* repair clocks. They are frequently employed by jewellers, antique shops or places devoted strictly to repairing clocks and watches.

The clockmakers of the present must be able to read blueprints and instructions for numerous types of clocks and time pieces that vary from antique clocks to modern time pieces in order to fix and make clocks or watches. The trade requires fine motor coordination as clockmakers must frequently work on devices with small gears and fine machinery, as well as an appreciation for the original art form. As is evident from this very short history of clocks and watches, over the centuries the items themselves have changed – almost out of recognition, but the importance of time-keeping has not. It is an area which provides a constant source of fascination and scientific discovery, still very much evolving today. We hope the reader enjoys this book.

The Story of Edward Howard *and the* First American Watch

THE American Watch, like practically every other great achievement of American inventors, was wrought out under discouragements that would have appalled ordinary men.

While Morse was struggling against the sickening disappointments of the telegraph, and Goodyear was undergoing privation in his search for the secret of curing India rubber, Edward Howard, with the assistance of capital furnished by friends, was struggling with the creation of the watch industry.

Edward Howard was apprenticed in 1829 to Aaron Willard, Jr., son of Aaron Willard, who was the youngest of three brothers, born in Grafton, Mass.

The Willards were noted for their fine clock work. Simon, the oldest, settled in

Roxbury in 1771 at the "Sign of the Clock." He made his first clock at the age of 13, and was the most ingenious of all the Willards. He made turret clocks for Boston, Philadelphia, New York and the University of Virginia. While in Virginia he became acquainted with Jefferson and Madison, with whom he corresponded for years. He made and set up the clocks in United States Senate and House. "He never considered profit, the quality of work being everything. His clocks, great and small, are just as good, after the lapse of a century, as when they left his hands."

Aaron Willard, Jr., learned the trade from his father, and to him Edward Howard was apprenticed in 1829. Young Howard was a mechanical genius. Clockmaking was play for him. Some of the clocks that he made as a boy are as good to-day as when they were first put up. He made all kinds of clocks —for halls and churches, tower clocks, etc.

He was one of the finest workmen that ever lived. His "bent," as he says, was all for finer and more delicate mechanism. It was natural that he should consort with the best watchmakers he could find. Watchmaking fascinated him. He studied it; saw its weaknesses and dreamed of overcoming them and of revolutionizing the watch industry of the world.

Think of the immortal nerve of that raw American boy who had never been outside of a little Massachusetts town, yet who dared aspire to better the work of the master craftsmen of Europe with ten generations of watchmaking behind them. Watchmaking ranked with the fine arts. It had its history, its traditions, its guilds and its court subsidies.

Howard, writing in later life of his early struggles, remarks: "One difficulty I found was that watchmaking did not exist in the United States as an industry. There were watchmakers, so called, at that time, and there are great numbers of the same kind now, but they never made a watch; their business being only to clean and repair."

He further says: "I knew from experience that there was no proper system employed in making watches. The work was all done by hand. Now handwork is superior

HOWARD
WATCH
MAKER

in many of the arts because it allows variation according to the individuality of the worker.

"But in the exquisitely fine wheels and screws and pinions that make up the parts of a watch, the less variation the better. Understand that some of these parts are so fine as to be almost invisible to the naked eye. A variation of one five-thousandth of an inch would throw the watch out altogether or make it useless as a timepiece. As I say, all of these minute parts were laboriously cut and filed out by hand, so it will readily be understood that in watches purporting to be of the same size and of the same makers there were no two alike, and there was no interchangeability of parts. Consequently it was 'cut and try.' A great deal of time was wasted and many imperfections resulted."

It was Howard's dream to overcome the imperfections by inventing automatic machines that would produce each part with absolute precision.

There's a childlike simplicity in the notes he has left about himself and his work.

This idea of automatic machines was daring and revolutionary enough in all conscience. Yet he says of it simply: "The development of the plan was the result of long thinking;" and further: "I came in for much ridicule from those to whom I confided it. They laughingly said, and I thought with some reason, that one of my machines, if I ever got it running, would be a greater marvel than the finest watch that ever was made.

"There was almost a superstitious belief in the necessity for handwork in making a watch movement. To those who criticized me for trying to do away with handwork I replied that I expected to make by hand the machines that were to make my watch parts, so it was handwork but one step removed."

Howard went into business for himself in 1840, risking all that he possessed and all that he could command from the few friends who believed in him. He determined to establish systematic watchmaking and to invent labor-saving machinery for producing perfect and interchangeable parts.

His first step was to build a small factory

in Roxbury, Mass.—the first watch factory in the New World.

Writing of this period he says: "It is almost needless to say that we met with many obstacles. We were told by importers and dealers in watches that we would never be able to carry out our plans and that our project would be an utter failure. Some of our friends even told us we were crazy to attempt such an undertaking. But we were Americans and had a sufficient quantity of the proverbial grit, and at least believed in ourselves even if others did not have so much faith.

"We could not import and use foreign help unacquainted with our methods and tools, so we had to instruct our men from the beginning. There were many times when we felt that the predictions of the importers would prove true, but perseverance conquered.

"The financial problem was a hard matter to solve as the unbelief in our success was universal. Frequently it was difficult to raise the money needed to get materials or pay our workmen. We struggled along for six years before the tide turned.

"Without the financial assistance of good friends in Boston, watchmaking would probably not have existed at the present time as an organized industry in the United States. This may seem to be a sweeping statement but no one can conceive the trials we endured. We hear about going through Purgatory but that must be a pleasure compared with what we experienced at that time.

"We were trying to establish under one roof an industry embracing a dozen distinct trades. Such a thing had never been done before and we were still further handicapped in our undertaking by having inexperienced assistants. We had to teach ourselves first and then teach others. Our progress was slow and expensive; and there was much bad work that we had to throw away.

"Our first watch was made to run for eight days, but was discarded because the mainspring was too long and cumbersome.

"We did not know how to make a jewel, or a dial or to do proper watch gilding or to produce a mirror polish on steel. We had to study and work over these operations until after many attempts one at last would be successful.

"We had to invent all the tools to make the different parts. After being designed or invented they had to be made in the factory by our own machinists in order to have them perfect and durable. Attempts were made to have them made outside but it was impossible to get them constructed carefully and of the exact and uniform sizes needed.

"It was nearly three years before the establishment had fairly and fully started in the business of making watches, and then we found that we would need ten times as much room, so we set about building a very much larger factory at Waltham, Mass."

The expenses of this new factory were greater than was anticipated. The constant experimenting, the cost of working models, the spoiled materials, rejected work, the building of new machines and the comparatively small marketable output, a thousand discouragements and the antagonism of the entire watch and jewelry trade finally brought matters to a crisis and Howard saw ruin staring him in the face. Some of his associates complained that he was too scrupulous about the perfection of the watches that left his hands.

He says on this point: "Friends turned from me saying I was not practical. Workmen who left me or were discharged complained that I was exacting and expected the impossible because I would not tolerate a botch of any kind. I would rather break up a watch movement than have it go out imperfect. My standard for every watch that bore my name was that it be fit to present to the President of the United States. They had me quite humbled and ashamed with the thought that I was not fair to those interested, but I could not bring myself to do otherwise.

"Of course, men who were looking at the financial side could not feel as I did about my watch. They could not understand that the watch was the end I sought, that I would give everything I possessed, even life itself, to see all work out as I had planned."

This was the temper of the man as attested by all who knew him. It was currently believed at the time that Howard was the model for the character of Owen Warland in Nathaniel Hawthorne's short story, "The Artist of the Beautiful."

Howard was a workman of astonishing dexterity and the highest ideals. His venture created a great deal of stir, because of its apparent impracticability, and Hawthorne, living in Concord at the time, could not have failed to hear a great deal of it. The story was published in June, 1844, only a year or so after the first Howard watch was completed.

The Howard factory failed in 1857.

The plant, tools and machinery were taken over by men in Waltham and became the nucleus of the great industry there and incidentally the parent of watch factories in other parts of the country.

Howard's characteristic comment on this state of affairs was this: "I had to begin at the bottom and make all tools anew. I returned to my old factory at Roxbury, founded a new company with the understanding that I was to have my way about the quality of watches that bore the name HOWARD."

How he succeeded is a matter of history.

The output was limited but a Howard watch was a prized possession. Men paid $500 for them in the early sixties.

A prominent citizen of Philadelphia (a retired business man) wrote the Howard factory recently that he had personally carried a Howard watch for fifty years and that its variation to-day is not more than one second in twenty-four hours, or one second in eighty-six thousand.

Howard had perfected his marvellous automatic machinery for the making of the delicate watch parts so that of a thousand pieces one would be exactly like the other.

Three thousand two hundred patents granted by the Patent Office at Washington in the field of watch and clock invention are directly or indirectly due to his initiative.

He had made the first practical application of the stem-winding mechanism designed in a crude form by a London watchmaker in 1750.

Now comes the most important work that Edward Howard accomplished in the direction of timekeeping accuracy.

We have noted his complaint of the variation of individual parts made by hand and learned how he overcame that difficulty.

Next, we find him making a curious discovery, viz.: "Every watch has its individuality. Pick out and put together two sets of absolutely perfect and identical parts made by machinery that does not vary one twenty-thousandth of an inch, run them under exactly the same conditions, and each watch will vary slightly from the other and from the standard."

He had gotten away from individuality in the parts only to meet it again in the assembled movement. And that discovery was the beginning of the Howard constructive adjustment that is obtained in no other watch factory to this day.

It takes months to adjust a Howard watch, notwithstanding the fact that it is a better timekeeper than the usual high-grade watch when it is first put together. The Howard requirements are higher.

It is run and timed for a period on its face, on its back, in different positions. Then in an oven with intense heat, then in a refrigerator under extreme cold. Accurate record being kept of its performance from day to day.

When it varies it goes into the hands of an expert who overhauls it until he finds the cause of variation, corrects it—then the watch starts on its test performance all over again.

The result is that the Howard adjustment when completed is good for fifty years (barring accidents or violence). It will stand more jolt and jar than any other watch, being adjusted to vibration as well as change of temperature.

Howard thought more of his scientific adjustment than anything else he accomplished. He left minute instructions and provisions for its continuance along with certain data that he would never divulge during his lifetime nor trust even with the patent authorities, though it is likely the matters were not in their nature subject to patent right protection.

Previous to 1853 the American markets were controlled by Swiss and English makers and there was much prejudice against Howard's product.

Howard writes in 1850: "Americans

have never been free from a snobbishness that loves to display a foreign trade mark. Just as the footman is more lordly than his master, so the tradesman is more snobbish than his customer."

But in spite of the ban on Howard by importers and retail jewelers, he was instrumental in driving the Swiss watches from the country.

In 1866 American watches were extensively introduced into London. The English watch industry declined. English makers came here and bought American watch machinery but could do little with it. Howard forced the Swiss makers to buy American machinery and Swiss watches are made on American machines to-day.

There is a record for you! That half-baked Roxbury boy with his *idea*—the scoff and butt of his companions—a lad that couldn't have got a job at the bench with the Swiss makers—yet he broke the back of a world industry and brought the richest guilds in Europe to Massachusetts begging for his machinery that they might continue their trade. And yet there are American jewelers who offer Swiss watches as a superior imported article.

Years later, the Howard factory was again removed to Waltham—the scene of its early failure—where it is now established as a splendid enterprise and a monument to a man who believed in himself; who countenanced no sham in his work and who lived to make the finest watches in the world.

In 1864, when the premium on gold put the price of watches so high, Secretary Stanton showed President Lincoln an expensive Swiss watch. Lincoln opened the back cap, examined the movement curiously and returned it to Stanton saying: "I reckon that's a Swiss watch, but it was made with American machines."

"It's a more elaborate watch than we make in this country, Mr. Lincoln," Stanton said.

"Yes," replied Lincoln, "it reminds me of the boy who wanted to teach his grandmother to suck eggs."

Lincoln carried a Howard.

Howard Watches in 18 and 14 K. Solid Gold and Gold Filled Cases

16 SIZE

Prices in Eighteen-Karat Extra Heavy Gold Cases

Grade	Hunting		Open-Face	
23 Jewels, adj. to Heat, Cold, 5 Positions and Isochronism. (RAILROAD STANDARD)	# 12 P. P. # 13 E.T.	$170.00	# 22 P. P. # 23 E.T.	$155.00
21 " " " " " 5 " " " "	Open-Face only		# 122 P. P. # 123 E.T.	140.00
19 " " " " " 5 " " " "	# 512 P. P. # 513 E.T.	145.00	# 522 P. P. # 523 E.T.	130.00
17 " " " " " 5 " " " "	# 212 P. P. # 213 E.T.	130.00	# 222 P. P. # 223 E.T.	115.00
17 " " " " " 3 " " " Double Roller	# 912 P. P. # 913 E.T.	120.00	# 922 P. P. # 923 E.T.	105.00
17 " " " " " 3 " " " Single Roller	# 312 P. P. # 313 E.T.	115.00		

16 SIZE

Prices in Fourteen-Karat Extra Heavy Gold Cases

Grade	Hunting		Open-Face	
23 Jewels, adj. to Heat, Cold, 5 Positions and Isochronism, (RAILROAD STANDARD)	# 10 P. P. # 20 E.T.	$150.00	# 15 P. P. # 25 E.T.	$140.00
21 " " " " " 5 " " " "	Open-Face only		# 115 P. P. # 125 E.T.	125.00
19 " " " " " 5 " " " "	# 510 P. P. # 520 E.T.	125.00	# 515 P. P. # 525 E.T.	115.00
17 " " " " " 5 " " " "	# 210 P. P. # 220 E.T.	110.00	# 215 P. P. # 225 E.T.	100.00
17 " " " " " 3 " " " Double Roller	# 910 P. P. # 920 E.T.	100.00	# 915 P. P. # 925 E.T.	90.00
17 " " " " " 3 " " " Single Roller	# 310 P. P. # 320 E.T.	95.00		

16 SIZE

Prices in Fourteen-Karat Heavy Gold Cases

Grade	Hunting		Open-Face	
23 Jewels, adj. to Heat, Cold, 5 Positions and Isochronism, (RAILROAD STANDARD)	# 30 P. P. # 40 E.T.	$135.00	# 35 P. P. # 45 E.T.	$125.00
21 " " " " " 5 " " " "	Open-Face only		# 135 P. P. # 145 E.T.	110.00
19 " " " " " 5 " " " "	# 530 P. P. # 540 E.T.	105.00	# 535 P. P. # 545 E.T.	95.00
17 " " " " " 5 " " " "	# 230 P. P. # 240 E.T.	95.00	# 235 P. P. # 245 E.T.	85.00
17 " " " " " 3 " " " Double Roller	# 930 P. P. # 940 E.T.	85.00	# 935 P. P. # 945 E.T.	75.00
17 " " " " " 3 " " " Single Roller	# 330 P. P. # 340 E.T.	80.00		

16 SIZE

Prices of Fourteen-Karat "Carvel" Watch

Furnished in this Grade of Movement only

	Open-Face
17 Jewels, adj. to Heat, Cold, 3 Positions and Isochronism, Double Roller, ...	# 905 P. P. $ 55.00

16 SIZE

Prices in Jas. Boss and Crescent Gold Filled Cases

Grade	Hunting		Open-Face	
23 Jewels, adj. to Heat, Cold, 5 Positions and Isochronism, (RAILROAD STANDARD)	# 50 P. P. # 60 E.T.	$ 92.50	# 55 P. P. # 65 E.T.	$ 90.00
21 " " " " " 5 " " " "	Open-Face only		# 155 P. P. # 165 E.T.	75.00
19 " " " " " 5 " " " "	# 550 P. P. # 560 E.T.	62.50	# 555 P. P. # 565 E.T.	60.00
17 " " " " " 5 " " " "	# 250 P. P. # 260 E.T.	52.50	# 255 P. P. # 265 E.T.	50.00
17 " " " " " 3 " " " Double Roller	# 950 P. P. # 960 E.T.	42.50	# 955 P. P. # 965 E.T.	40.00
17 " " " " " 3 " " " Single Roller	# 350 P. P. # 360 E.T.	37.50		

16 SIZE

Prices in Jas. Boss and Crescent Gold Filled, Swing Ring, Dustproof Cases

Jewels	Description	Case Nos.	Open-Face
23	Jewels, adj. to Heat, Cold, 5 Positions and Isochronism, (RAILROAD STANDARD)	# 75 P. P. / # 85 E.T.	$ 90.00
21	" " " " " 5 " " " "	# 175 P. P. / # 185 E.T.	75.00
19	" " " " " 5 " " " "	# 575 P. P. / # 585 E.T.	60.00
17	" " " " " 5 " " " "	# 275 P. P. / # 285 E.T.	50.00
17	" " " " " 3 " " " Double Roller	# 975 P. P. / # 985 E.T.	40.00

Sixteen-size, Open Face Lever Setting Howard Watches—23, 21, 19 and 17 Jewels, Five Position Adjusted—are officially certified and adopted as Railroad Standard by the Time Inspectors of 180 of the leading railroads of America. The finest Railroad Watches in the world.

12 SIZE EXTRA THIN MODEL

Heavy Eighteen-Karat Gold Cases

Jewels	Description	Case Nos.	Hunting	Case Nos.	Open-Face
21	Jewels, adj. to Heat, Cold, 5 Positions and Isochronism,	# 812 P. P. / # 813 E.T.	$155.00	# 822 P. P. / # 823 E.T.	$140.00
19	" " " " " 5 " " "	# 612 P. P. / # 613 E.T.	125.00	# 622 P. P. / # 623 E.T.	110.00
17	" " " " " 3 " " "	# 712 P. P. / # 713 E.T.	105.00	# 722 P. P. / # 723 E.T.	90.00

12 SIZE

Fourteen-Karat Gold Cases

	Hunting		Open-Face	
21 Jewels, adj. to Heat, Cold, 5 Positions and Isochronism,	#830 P. P. #840 E.T.	$135.00	#835 P. P. #845 E.T.	$125.00
19 " " " " " 5 " " "	#630 P. P. #640 E.T.	105.00	#635 P. P. #645 E.T.	95.00
17 " " " " " 3 " " "	#730 P. P. #740 E.T.	85.00	#735 P. P. #745 E.T.	75.00

12 SIZE

Jas. Boss and Crescent Gold Filled Cases

	Hunting		Open-Face	
21 Jewels, adj. to Heat, Cold, 5 Positions and Isochronism,	#850 P. P. #860 E.T.	$ 92.50	#855 P. P. #865 E.T.	$ 90.00
19 " " " " " 5 " " "	#650 P. P. #660 E.T.	62.50	#655 P. P. #665 E.T.	60.00
17 " " " " " 3 " " "	#750 P. P. #760 E.T.	42.50	#755 P. P. #765 E.T.	40.00

12 SIZE

Crescent "Cavetto" Gold Filled Cases

	Hunting		Open-Face	
21 Jewels, adj. to Heat, Cold, 5 Positions and Isochronism,	#850C P. P. #860C E.T.	$ 92.50	#855C P. P. #865C E.T.	$ 90.00
19 " " " " " 5 " " "	#650C P. P. #660C E.T.	62.50	#655C P. P. #665C E.T.	60.00
17 " " " " " 3 " " "	#750C P. P. #760C E.T.	42.50	#755C P. P. #765C E.T.	40.00

www.ingramcontent.com/pod-product-compliance
Lightning Source LLC
LaVergne TN
LVHW041929090826
845145LV00017B/2780

* 9 7 8 1 4 7 3 3 2 8 4 9 5 *